SIR ALFRED MUNNINGS 1878–1959

An appreciation of the artist and a selection of his paintings
by STANLEY BOOTH

The night cometh
when no man shall work

SOTHEBY'S PUBLICATIONS

LIST OF COLOUR ILLUSTRATIONS

INTRODUCTION

*'To be a great painter you mustn't be pious but rather a little wicked
and entirely a man of the World'*

JOHN RUSKIN

SIR ALFRED MUNNINGS, KCVO, PRA, a truly self-made man, was one of the great English characters of this century. A provincial painter, with no expectations of becoming a Royal Academician, let alone President of the Royal Academy, by sheer merit he achieved a world-wide reputation and a place among the best painters of the day. This book has been compiled to show the breadth of his artistic talent.

Munnings's output was prodigious and although many of his works have frequently been reproduced he kept no detailed records. It has, therefore, been necessary to seek out the whereabouts of many hundreds of his pictures spread throughout the world. Though the final choice of those reproduced in this book has been determined to some extent by their accessibility for photography, a selection has been made, arranged in chronological order as far as possible, which demonstrates his great versatility, from his early poster work and first Royal Academy pictures to his later commissioned work and the horse-racing and race-course scenes, for which he is perhaps best remembered today. The pictures themselves speak for Munnings's artistic skill, his inventiveness and originality, and his ability to capture a fleeting moment. They show that as a painter of horses he worthily carried on the tradition of Ben Marshall and George Stubbs, both of whom he greatly admired.

Always a controversial figure, Munnings's speech at the Academy banquet in 1949, which was broadcast 'live', created a furore at the time and brought him much notoriety. Unsophisticated, no politician and never prepared to trim his sails, his attack on contemporary artistic trends was made in his characteristic blunt, forthright, opinionated, and perhaps tactless, manner and stoked up fires with the many enemies he made, the embers of which still glow today. 'As I am President and have the right of the Chair, allow me to speak. I shall not be here next year, thank God.', he said, raising his voice against interruptions. 'I find myself President of a body of men who are what I call shilly-shallying. They feel there is something in this so-called modern art . . . I myself would rather have – excuse me my Lord Archbishop – a damned bad failure, a bad muddy old picture where someone has tried to do something, to set down what they have seen, than all this affected juggling . . . these violent blows at nothing . . . foolish drolleries. If you paint a tree, for God's sake try to make it look like a tree and if you paint a sky try and make it look like a sky . . . there has been a foolish interruption to all efforts in art, helped by foolish men writing in the press encouraging all this damned nonsense, putting all these younger men out of their stride. I am right.'

The newspapers gave the speech priority and the Royal Academy had never had such a press, whilst to the majority of the wide radio audience provided by the BBC it was a new experience and a breath of fresh air to hear someone in authority express himself in such a down-to-earth manner. Munnings had certainly gone further than any President of the Royal Academy in bringing controversy about art into millions of homes and he almost certainly echoed the unspoken views of the majority of his listeners. To hear the recording of that speech now, the overriding impression is of the sincerity of feeling behind the words. His outspokenness and vehemence were entirely in character, as was the courage needed to speak his mind on such an occasion and to such a wide audience.

Alfred Munnings was born of old East Anglian farming stock on 8 October 1878, the second son of John Munnings, miller, of Mendham, Suffolk. He revealed artistic talent at a very early

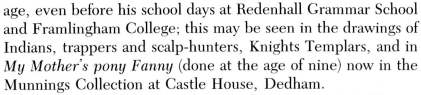

An early drawing of fishing boats

One of Munnings's boyhood drawings of Indian scalp-hunters

age, even before his school days at Redenhall Grammar School and Framlingham College; this may be seen in the drawings of Indians, trappers and scalp-hunters, Knights Templars, and in *My Mother's pony Fanny* (done at the age of nine) now in the Munnings Collection at Castle House, Dedham.

Leaving Framlingham at the age of fourteen and a half it was all but settled that young Alfred should go to work for a publishing firm in Norwich, when by chance his drawings and paintings were shown to a friend of the family. He was enthusiastic about Alfred's work and declared that the boy must not go into the publishing world but into lithography. This friend told Munnings's father about the two leading firms in Norwich; in the event Alfred was bound apprentice for the term of six years to the firm of Page Brothers, his father paying a premium of forty pounds. Working alongside six lithographic artists from nine in the morning to seven at night, and one o'clock on Saturdays, his weekly wage began at two shillings and sixpence rising to the sum of one pound ten shillings after several years. When work was over he used to walk straight down to the Norwich School of Art, studying there until nine each evening.

Munnings spent six years at the School of Art and for the greater part of that time worked under, and was greatly influenced by, Miss Gertrude Offord, a well known watercolour painter of flowers and whose name was frequently in the Academy catalogues of the 'eighties and 'nineties. He enjoyed and found exciting the painting of watercolours, and tried to send in six works each year, first to the Royal Institute of Painters in Watercolours and later, when elected a member, to the Royal Watercolour Society. This he continued to do well into the 'twenties when he began to find the change from one medium to another too big an interruption in his painting of large oils.

During his six years of apprenticeship Munnings came to the attention of John Shaw Tomkins, a director of A. J. Caley & Son, Chocolate Manufacturers, who became his earliest patron and greatly encouraged him. The ideas for posters, for chocolate-box tops, advertisements for crackers and Christmas novelties were worked out by Page Brothers for Caley's and, as Munnings learned more and more at the School of Art and his drawings improved, he became the artist responsible for this work. He was beginning to sell his work at the exhibitions of the

A prize-winning poster design

A stone-breaker in Cornwall

Norwich Art Circle and Tomkins would buy his best water-colours and later commissioned Munnings to paint his father.

Tomkins took Munnings on his first visit abroad going, by way of The Hague, Amsterdam and Berlin, to the Leipzig Fair where A. J. Caley & Son had a display stand for which Munnings designed and painted posters on the spot. He was eighteen at the time and it was in Amsterdam that he saw a small painting of a little girl in a pale blue overall, wearing a black stocking cap, sitting on a sand dune. This gave him the idea for his delightful painting *Stranded* (4), the original of which is in the Bristol Art Gallery, dated 1898 but painted in 1897. This and *Pike-fishing in January* (5) were accepted and hung by the Royal Academy in 1899, the first of his two hundred and eighty-nine pictures to be hung in the Royal Academy Summer Exhibitions up to 1959.

The day he heard of the acceptance of his first Academy pictures was also the day Munnings had his first taste of the racing scene which was to figure so largely in his career in later

A drawing of one of Munnings's cousins

Munnings's brother, Charles, who died in his twenties in South Africa

years. He was taken to Bungay Races by a friend who had persuaded him to take a day off work to celebrate the occasion. Later he was to write 'I saw the thoroughbred horses and jockeys in bright silk colours, going off down the course. The peaceful School of Art, the smelly artists' room at Page Brothers faded away and I began to live!'

Munnings showed his independence when, at the age of twenty, after finishing his apprenticeship, he turned down an offer of five pounds a week – a large sum then – to continue working for Page Brothers. With his small savings he elected to seek his way as a professional artist and, returning to Mendham,

he bought for fifty pounds a carpenter's shop which was to become his studio. One marvels at the courage and tenacity of this young man of twenty who, within months of taking this major decision, had lost the sight of his right eye in an accident (a wound from a briar when lifting a dog over a hedge). In his autobiography he wrote: 'I wasn't allowed to use my remaining eye for months afterwards, and when I began to do so I could not judge distances, and poured water on the cloth, missing the glass. I went to paint, and my brush either hit the canvas before I knew it was there, or was not touching it. Mostly it was the latter, and I found myself making stroke after stroke in the air, nearer and nearer, until I touched the painted surface. A long time elapsed before I became used to this, and even now I often make a stroke in the air which doesn't arrive on the canvas, or make another which lands too violently. This has been a handicap to me always, and cramps my style – shortens my stride, so to speak. What wouldn't I give to see with two eyes again!'

Savings dwindled fast as Munnings's carpenter's shop grew into a studio, and, although he lived at home for a while, he could not exist on what paintings he might chance to sell, so he continued for some years to work free-lance on poster design and advertising work, much of it for Shaw Tomkins of Caley's. In between this work he pursued his ambition to paint horses, village characters, hunting scenes and landscapes. Gradually through the Norwich Art Circle and Boswells, a firm of art dealers in that city, his pictures became known and were sold at modest prices.

Munnings soon established his complete independence by leaving home and renting rooms at Shearing's Farm in Mendham and then, on the strength of his income from his free-lance poster work and the sales of his pictures, he also rented rooms in Norwich to establish a base there. It was from these rooms in Norwich that he began to develop and extend a boisterous social life which gave full rein to his extrovert nature and his marked talents as an entertainer. He would be the central performer at parties which he organised and, with his penchant for stylish, if unusual, dress it was said that he could equally well have made his way on the stage. Whether at a private party with his friends, at a select gathering, at the local village hall, or later giving an impromptu performance to the studio staff and technicians of the BBC after a television appearance, he could keep his audience enthralled as a raconteur or by the vigour of his rendering of the ballads which he wrote himself.

Apart from two short periods of study and painting at Julian's atelier in Paris in 1902 and 1903 (a number of works from which periods are at Castle House), Munnings stayed at Mendham for six years, until 1904, when he moved to Swainsthorpe, some five miles south of Norwich. Here, for ten pounds a year, he rented part of a farmhouse, Church Farm, from a relative, and built a new studio. He lived and worked at Swainsthorpe for several years. It was from here that he made his expeditions into the Ringland Hills in Norfolk, and to Hoxne, on the River Waveney in Suffolk. He travelled with the string of seven or eight nondescript horses and ponies and a donkey that he had acquired, together with a blue painted caravan, and a flat cart for his canvases and painting materials. His man, Bob, was in charge of the whole procession, helped by a gypsy boy called Shrimp. All these were his models, when for weeks at a time he worked out-of-doors, in what to him was the right environment. Munnings related how in 1909 he worked from the beginning of May until the middle of July in Ringland and Costessey. 'The caravan loaded with pictures and belongings, drawn as before by the two white ponies, rumbled out on

A painting done at Julian's atelier, rue de Dragon, Paris

to the road, followed by the other ponies – the packed-up cart bringing up the rear. With myself in the lead, we left Ringland, making for our headquarters at Swainsthorpe. At Church Farm the van was unloaded, pictures placed in the studio, fresh canvases put in, rolls of unstretched canvas, more brushes, more paints, more oil and turpentine, and all things needful to the painter. Spending only one night there, we started at five next morning in the same order of march, the caravan leading, on the 30-mile journey to Spring Farm at Hoxne. In this far-off, remote district in a sylvan setting, we had found a happy valley – an Arcadia.' Many of his subjects were repeated in several different versions but from these expeditions came such notable pictures as *The Coming Storm* (21), *Ponies in a Sandpit* (20), *The Ford* and the series of gravelpit scenes, of which '*Augereau*' is an example.

Of horses Munnings wrote 'Although they have given me much trouble and many sleepless nights, they have been my supporters, friends – my destiny in fact. Looking back at my life, interwoven with theirs – painting them, feeding them, riding them, thinking about them – I hope that I have learned something of their ways. I have never ceased trying to understand them.' He bought his first horse in his early twenties at Mendham and from that time he was rarely without one or more; not the nondescript ponies used as models in his early works, but thoroughbred hunters, models for many of his paintings, ridden both by Munnings and his wife. Although he enjoyed hunting he enjoyed still more long quiet rides along country lanes when he relaxed, was good-tempered and really happy. While his wife was out hunting he would often be far away on a thirty- or forty-mile ride taking a whole day in which to do it; and the next day he would be off on another long ride on a different horse. 'I was like a thirsty man let loose in a cellar: I became drunk with riding' he wrote. 'Anarchist', 'Rufus', 'Cheena', 'Winter Rose' and 'Cherrybounce', the last two of which he bred, and many more horses figure largely in his work and his relaxation. At the start of the Second World War he had seventeen in his stables and in the paddocks at Castle House, and up to the last few months of his life he was a familiar figure riding in the lanes around Dedham.

In the late summer of 1910 Munnings made his first visit to Cornwall, to see the country and coast which attracted many artists. He was anxious to make the acquaintance of the then famous Newlyn School, a founder of which was Stanhope

A drawing of a friend

Forbes, RA. Forbes had gathered around him a circle which included Harold and Laura Knight, both of whom were to become Munnings's lifelong friends. This first visit to Cornwall was short, but he was welcomed into the community and, finding the scenery, so different from his familiar Norfolk and Suffolk, immensely to his liking he made further visits in 1911 and established himself towards the end of that year with stables and a studio at Lamorna Cove, a few miles from Newlyn.

His mother wrote in her diary at that time 'Alfred's mare and Taffy, his dog, gone to Cornwall today. Now I feel I have lost Alfred. The mare and the dog were the last links between us.'

Munnings had kept on his Swainsthorpe studio, however, and Dame Laura Knight in her autobiography *Oil Paint and Grease Paint* wrote of him: 'One year A. J. invited Harold and me to go and see his work at Swainsthorpe. His studio was full of canvases of all sizes. Many of the ideas and starts we saw then have since become famous pictures.

'We went over to Norwich for the night and dined with him at the Maid's Head Hotel. We sat in the bar-parlour afterwards sipping port at a shiny mahogany table. To look at A.J. in those surroundings took you back 150 years; he fitted into the antiquity; even his clothes had a cut that belonged to the past. I unfortunately infuriated him on this occasion by taking a bath and thus adding a shilling to his account, nothing compared to the sum he had expended for the wines he had lavished on us the night before. "All this washing," he said. "What do you want a bath for?"

'Several people in one; for a flash a poet, a supersensitive creature of refined tastes and instincts, of culture; one moment canny, the next plunged back into great generosity and lavish extravagance. He could be the best of hosts and, the best of entertainers, as he was that night – there is no better guide to old England than A.J.'

It was from Lamorna that Munnings made his expeditions to Hampshire where, in 1913, he had discovered in the gypsy hop-pickers a wealth of models. His pictures of gypsy life are among his best works and such notable examples as *Departure of the Hop-pickers* (National Gallery of Victoria, Melbourne; 26) and *Gypsy Life* (Aberdeen Art Gallery; 33) did much to establish his name and fortune. 'Of all my painting experiences, none were so alluring and colourful as those visits spent amongst the gypsy hop-pickers in Hampshire each September. More glamour and excitement were packed into those six weeks than a painter could well contend with. I still have visions of brown faces, black hair, earrings, black hats and black skirts; of lithe figures of women and children, of men with lurcher dogs and horses of all kinds. I still recall the never-ceasing din around their fires as the sun went down, with blue smoke curling up amongst the trees. I think of crowded days of work – too swiftly gone.'

When the First World War broke out Munnings was rejected on two occasions by the army because of his sight, but

A sketch of a girl for 'Tagg's Island'

in 1917, with the help of a friend, he got a lowly job caring for remounts at Calcot Park near Reading. When he left Lamorna, Laura Knight said of him 'His extraordinary vitality, his joy in his work – none of us could forget him. He was a fighter. He fought the wind that shivered his easel and canvas. He fought the heat and the cold. He fought the shifting sun and the changing shadows.'

Early in 1918 Munnings was sent to France as an official war

A preparatory drawing for the portrait of General Seely

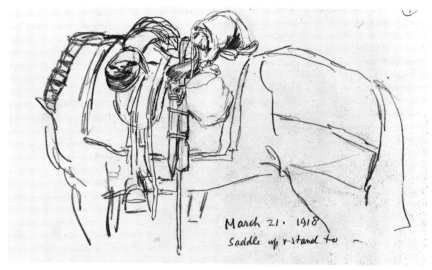

A First World War sketch

artist attached to the Canadian Cavalry Brigade under the command of General Jack Seely (later Lord Mottistone). Years later in his book *My Horse Warrior,* Lord Mottistone described his meeting with Munnings: 'It was in this part of the world [the section of the front near the Omignon river] that Warrior first made friends with a very remarkable person. He turned up one morning in plain clothes, in this bleak area, where for months no human being had been seen in anything but French, English or German uniform. Of course it had never been the intention of the Canadian authorities that Munnings should join us in the front line, but this whimsical and gallant soul thought that this was just the best place in which to be. And so it turned out, for by common consent his paintings and drawings of the Canadian horses, close to the front line, are some of the most brilliant things he has ever done.

'As I rode back from the front line one cold morning, covered with mud, I met this strange apparition in civilian clothes. Munnings said: "Come along, I want to paint you." So Warrior and I had to stand stock still while the eminent man drew us.

'It was bitterly cold day and painting a portrait in the open air must have been both difficult and unpleasant. The frost of the night before had left a thin crust on the top of the ground, and through this the unfortunate Munnings kept breaking into the mud underneath until I had him mounted on some duck-boards. Moreover, I could only spare him little more than an

hour and kept producing my watch and telling him how many minutes he had left.

'The portrait was finished in the afternoon with my orderly taking my place on Warrior, adorned in one of my spare caps and tunics.

'The background to the picture, which is now in Canada, at a distance of about three thousand five hundred yards, was German territory. Probably that fact would have deterred most artists from choosing such a place in which to paint a portrait. Not so Munnings; he seemed to think that it added greatly to its interest.'

This painting of General Seely on horseback proved to be an important milestone, if not the turning-point, in Munnings's career. As he himself wrote 'I have often wondered had there been no 1914–18 War whether painting people on horseback would have absorbed the greater part of my efforts in the years that followed. Starting with portraits of General Seely, Geoffrey Brook and the rest, which were shown with the Canadian War Records at the Academy, my next was a portrait of Lord Athlone in uniform on horseback. Being a good likeness, I sent it to the Royal Academy, where it was hung in the first room. This led to many commissions, which continued to the outbreak of the last War.'

These paintings demonstrated Munnings's ability to paint the rider's portrait as skilfully as the horse, and assured him of a flow of equestrian commissions which brought him money and fame and took him into a society and into great houses to an extent that would have been beyond his wildest imagination as a young man. With his sturdy independent character and lack of affectation he made no attempt to be other than himself, and was welcomed as a friend and an entertaining personality. From Kirby Hall, Melton Mowbray, where he had gone to paint Robert Strawbridge, an American who had been Master of the Cottesmore Hunt, he wrote to his wife 'Then that night I'm blessed if they didn't dine here!! Prince of Wales, Prince Henry and only Mr & Mrs Strawbridge and myself to meet them. And then I'm blessed if I didn't have to do my ballad *Anthony Bell* after dinner for them.'

In 1919 Munnings took what he described as the main decision of his life, the purchase of Castle House in Dedham – 'the house of my dreams' – where he lived until his death in 1959, except for a break during the Second World War when the army occupied Castle House and he and Lady Munnings went to live at Withypool, on Exmoor. He kept possession of his Swainsthorpe studio and had it moved to Castle House, where it still stands.

In March 1920 Alfred Munnings married Violet McBride, who was herself a horsewoman of renown and who had won the Gold Cup at Olympia, as well as many other prizes. Astute, shrewd and with a firm belief in her husband as a great artist, she was a tremendous help to Munnings in his career, attending to all his business matters and always promoting his interests. However she herself said that 'He was never such a good artist after he married me. He had establishments to keep up and more expenses to meet. It meant painting for money.' Certainly one gets the impression from his letters and from his autobiography that during the twenty years to 1940, when he travelled extensively in Europe, America and in the United Kingdom on painting commissions, he was always homesick for Dedham and the freedom to paint landscapes. He wrote 'After the first World War I was receiving letters asking me to paint somebody on a horse. Opening such letters, too often I gave way to a burst of petulant rage. "Oh, damn it, no!" said my independent self: "bother these commissions!" Then conscience – or was it my cautious self? – stepped in and said, "You can't throw good money away." Then I would write and accept the offer – fit the job in, so to speak – which was really the only thing to do. Better men than I spent their lives in painting commissioned pictures – do we not read how Sir Joshua in one of his busy years had over one hundred sitters? – but, for all

A pencil drawing of 'Son-in-law'

Sketches of ponies

Does the Subject Matter?
Sir John Rothenstein (then Director of the Tate Gallery), Humphrey Brooke
and Professor Mavrogordato examining a piece of 'contemporary' sculpture,
with Munnings's dog, Toby, on the right. This painting was shown at the
Royal Academy Summer Exhibition in 1956

that, I wanted to be painting the English scene.' For his retrospective exhibition in the Diploma Gallery of the Royal Academy in 1956 he insisted on 'not too many of those commissioned pictures'. His other great love was the racing scene. In the informal studies of horses and in particular his studies of the start at Newmarket, his ability to capture movement is unsurpassed.

Munnings was elected President of the Royal Academy in 1944 and was knighted in the same year, and in 1947 was appointed Knight Commander of the Royal Victorian Order. He did not really enjoy his Presidency, disliking intensely and finding burdensome the administrative and formal demands of the position. Although he ceased to be President in 1949 his banquet speech was not the last occasion on which he was to have a fling at modern art and cause acute embarrassment to the Academy in so doing. For the 1956 Summer Exhibition he sent in his lampoon on modern art entitled *Does the Subject Matter?*, for which no artistic merit could be claimed and which was akin to the poster work of his youth. The President, Sir Albert Richardson, wrote questioning the wisdom of 'AJ' in submitting this satirical picture, as much for the sake of Munnings's reputation as for the good name of the Academy. There ensued a voluminous and forthright correspondence typical of Munnings. To Richardson he wrote 'You have attacked, in biting phrases, work of modern architects. This gave many of us hope: now you tremble at a humorous picture aimed at modern art . . . and now that I am trying to hit back for tradition in paint, as you do in words, you object. For me it is a setback I least expected. After all, Sir, what in God's name is there to fear?'

To the catalogue entry of *Does the Subject Matter?* he had appended the lines:

And why not purchased for the State?
The State, alas, has come too late.
Because the subject's so profound
'Twas sold for twenty thousand pound!

but did not fail to broadcast that official scruples had changed his original 'Tate' to 'State'. The painting was hung inconspicuously but it became the season's most talked-of picture.

Alfred Munnings's fame is based on his painting of race-horses, yet before 1920, when he was elected an Associate of the Royal Academy, he had never painted a thoroughbred. It is, however, considered by many that his best work was produced in the period 1898 to 1914 with his recording of the English, and particularly the East Anglian, rural scene in all its aspects, skies, landcape, animals and human characters. Referring to these early efforts Munnings wrote 'There is no sophistry about them. They were done in my twenties, before I had learned the wiles and tricks which artists are supposed to know.' It could be said of his work that his training in lithography helped Munnings to develop his fluency; few artists have painted with greater speed and certainty. Yet the large number of studies and sketches he made bears witness to the thoroughness with which he tackled a subject.

In her book *Sporting Art*, Stella A. Walker summarises Munnings's place in art: 'His splendid studies of rough cobs and gypsy lads, the superlative expertise of *The Return from Ascot* with the Windsor greys, his studies of heavy-weight carriers with robust foxhunters and racing two-year-olds, were to bring to equestrian art of the twentieth century a brilliance of achievement not seen since the epoch of George Stubbs.' (A smaller version of the Ascot painting referred to bears the title *Their Majesties' return from Ascot*.

Studies of the head of 'Hyperion'

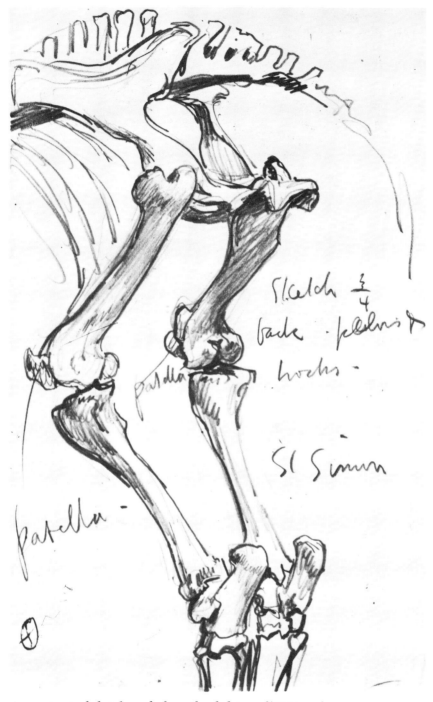

An anatomical sketch made from the skeleton of 'St Simon'

work, he was content to follow, perhaps lazily, the traditional pattern of the painter who works to commission, and who produces paintings to satisfy a public with little knowledge of art. It is certainly true that he was a painter the layman can understand, but then as he himself said 'What are pictures for? To fill a man's soul with admiration and sheer joy, not to bewilder and daze him.'

In all fields of creative endeavour natural ability and talent do not in themselves ensure success; sheer hard work and understanding of one's subject are essential ingredients. Munnings, having served an arduous apprenticeship, firmly believed in craftsmanship, schooling and the disciplines of the profession as the basic requirements for any artist. 'It is easier to imagine a painting being dashed off than it is for an artist to put his first solitary stroke on a canvas. If only those who knew their craft were allowed to do this, less canvases would be needed', he wrote.

People in most walks of life work under the influence of external pressures and often work the better for them but, in what must be a lonely profession, an artist generates his own pressures and, much as he may seek and want the approbation of the public and his fellow artists, in the final analysis he is his own judge. Of his own work Munnings wrote, 'Were I to write only of those of my pictures that satisfy me, my task would be a short one.' After a lifetime of exercising his own judgment it is perhaps not surprising that he was prepared to express his views strongly. From his earliest days he had done so; it was an essential part of the man that he had the courage to express his opinions even when they were contrary to the majority or those of the 'Establishment'.

Often throughout his life Munnings's behaviour and his pontifications made his friends quake for him, and he embarrassed would-be sympathisers. His faults, however, fade into insignificance when one considers the independence of character, the energy, the sheer willpower and determination that produced such a prodigious number of paintings, and overcame the disability of his sight together with the debilitating effect of gout suffered over many years. His attitude to modern art, whether well or badly expressed, was founded on his belief that much of it was a confidence trick on the public and not based on what he considered to be the essential virtues of craftsmanship and hard work. Munnings's nostalgia for the past and condemnation of twentieth-century 'progress' sprang from his great and

As an artist Munnings has not been without his detractors; criticisms of his talent as 'facile' and 'slight' have been made. It has been suggested that, while producing fashionable and lively

4th Race   **1 mile and a half**   Armlet: GREEN

3.30.—THE TELSCOMBE WELTER HANDICAP, a Plate of 300 sov.; the second to receive 60 sov. and the third 30 sov. out of the plate; for three-yrs-old and upwards; lowest handicap weight not less than 10st 7lb; a winner after the publication of the weights (August 12th, at noon) to carry 7lb extra; to be ridden by amateur riders duly qualified to ride in accordance with Rule 95 (li)—i.e., who hold a permit from the Stewards of the Jockey Club, or who are Officers on full pay serving in the Regular Forces—those who have never ridden a winner under any recognised Rules of Flat Racing allowed 5lb; entrance 1 sov., and 2 sov. more unless forfeit be declared to Messrs. Weatherby and Sons by August 17th; one mile and a half (20 entries, forfeit declared for 13).—Closed July 13th, 1943.

Age st lb

1—Duchess of Norfolk ......**BIRDFORTH** 6 11 9 sky blue & scarlet check, sky
   b h Flag of Truce—   *W. Smyth*   blue slvs, scarlet cap
       Winter Fruit

2—Maud Lady Fitzwilliam..**GROS BLEU** 5 11 7 green, black cross-belts, black
   ch h Messines or   *Warden*   cap
      Blue Moon—Goddle

3—Mr W. F. Stratton........**CLAY PIT** 5 11 3 yellow, blue cap
   b g Hastings—Birdline   *Owner*

4—Mr W. Hutchinson ...**STOCKBRIDGE** 4 11 0 gold, white cross-belts & cap
   br c Epigram—Palatial   *G. Allden*

5—Mr F. J. Abbott ....**TECHNIQUE** 5 10 9 green, white sleeves, black &
   ch h Casanova—Valuable *R. Maxwell*   white grtd cap

6—Mrs N. F. Oliver.........**THE EDITOR** 4 10 7 red, blue hoop
   b g Fonton—Headline   *G. Cutting*

7—Mrs C. D. Wilson............**EPIGRAPH** 5 10 7 blue, red & yellow hoop, hpd
   b g Epigram—Cordon   *Beeby*   cap

FURTHER MEETINGS AT BRIGHTON:—
TO-MORROW, AUGUST 28th.
SEPTEMBER 15th and 16th - - - **Wednesday and Thursday**

Sketches on a race-card

enduring love of the English countryside as well as his feeling that all that was beautiful in England was fast slipping away in a materialistic world where few cared.

Apart from his versatility as a painter, Munnings's sculpture was of a high order, as may be seen in *A Lieutenant of Hussars 1920* in Mells Church in Somerset. This bronze statue of Edward Horner on horseback was commissioned by Lady Horner as a memorial to her son who was killed in the First World War. Many years later Lord Hamilton of Dalzell, having seen this sculpture, commissioned Munnings, on behalf of the

A bronze sculpture of 'Brown Jack'

Jockey Club, to do a model for a bronze statuette of 'Brown Jack', winner of the Queen Alexandra States in six consecutive years, 1929 to 1934. It is placed at the top of the steps to the Royal Enclosure at Ascot on the day when the race for the Brown Jack Stakes is run. A casting may be seen at Castle House.

Munnings's achievement in a full and exciting life were rounded off by his remarkable autobiography, *An Artist's Life* (1950), *The Second Burst* (1951) and *The Finish* (1952). The three volumes of reminiscences and observations on the English scene cover some seventy years. His comments and descriptions taken from these three books provide the captions to many of the pictures reproduced here.

Though Munnings could be irascible and abrasive, his tremendous verve and warmth of character enriched the times in which he lived and the lives of those around him. Few artists have achieved fame and fortune in their own lifetime and fewer still have made the Nation the beneficiary of their life's work. Inscribed on his memorial tablet in the crypt of St Paul's Cathedral are the lines:

O friend, how very lovely are the things,
The English things, you helped us to perceive.

It had always been Munnings's wish that the pictures remaining in his possession and his estate should be left to the Nation for the encouragement of 'traditional' art. After his death in 1959 Lady Munnings, a considerable personality in her own right and always convinced of her husband's genius, worked towards this end. She established Castle House as an Art Museum. The house itself with its furnishings and the studios, all Sir Alfred's paintings which had remained in Lady Munnings's possession, some forty acres of land and investments were put into Trusts for this purpose and the house was opened to the public. Lady Munnings subsequently retired to her Chelsea home where Sir Alfred had a London studio, and where she died in October 1971.

Castle House, a mixture of Tudor and Georgian periods in a charming rural setting, has been completely restored in recent years. The pictures have been cleaned and a number of important acquisitions have been added to the collection, particularly paintings from Munnings's early period. The essential character and atmosphere of the Munnings's home has been retained and Sir Alfred's paintings are displayed in beautiful surroundings which present a fitting and living memorial to his work.

The grounds of Castle House

POSTER WORK
Carried out when Munnings was producing
designs for Messrs. Page Brothers of Norwich.
See also back cover.

1

RECLINING LADY

*Signed and dated 1898, 52 in by 78 in, Watercolour
and bodycolour*

2

DESIGN FOR COLMAN'S
MUSTARD

Signed, 12 in by 18 in, Watercolour and bodycolour

DANIEL TOMKINS AND HIS DOG

Painted 1898, Oil on canvas, 22 in by 26 in
Collection: The Sir Alfred Munnings Art Museum

STRANDED

Signed and dated '98, Oil on canvas, 18 in by 14 in
Exhibited Royal Academy 1899
Collection: City of Bristol Museum and Art Gallery

PIKE-FISHING IN JANUARY

*Signed and dated '98, Oil on canvas, 25 in
by 12 in
Exhibited Royal Academy 1899
Private collection*

Signed and dated 1901, Oil on canvas, 30 in by 50 in
Collection: Castle Museum, Norwich

Signed and dated 1902, Pencil, watercolour and bodycolour,
10¼ in by 16¼ in
Collection: Castle Museum, Norwich

Painted at Julian's atelier, rue du Dragon, Paris, 1902, Oil on canvas, 32⅛ in by 25¾ in Collection: The Sir Alfred Munnings Art Museum

A Gala Day

Signed and dated 1902, Oil on canvas, 20 in by 24 in
Exhibited Royal Academy 1903
Collection: Harris Museum and Art Gallery, Preston

THE LAST OF THE FAIR

Signed and dated 1903, Oil on canvas, 38 in by 45 in
Exhibited Royal Academy 1903
Collection: Harris Museum and Art Gallery, Preston

THE HORSE FAIR

Signed and dated 1904, Oil on canvas, 30¼ in by 50⅜ in
Collection: Castle Museum, Norwich

AT HETHERSETT RACES

Signed and dated 1904, Oil on canvas, 14 in by 18 in
Private collection

A White Slave

Signed and dated 1904, Oil on canvas, 39½ in by 59½ in
Exhibited Royal Academy 1905 as 'Leaving the Fair'
Collection: Art Gallery and Museum, Oldham

CHARLOTTE'S PONY

Signed and dated 1905, Oil on canvas, 25 in by 31 in
Exhibited Royal Academy 1907
Private collection

IDLE MOMENTS

Signed. Oil on canvas, 20 in by 24 in
Private collection

PORTRAIT OF NELLY GRAY

Signed and dated 1907, Oil on canvas, 29 in by 37 in
The Sir Alfred Munnings Art Museum

Signed and dated 1909, Oil on canvas, 19¼ in by 23¼ in
Private collection

HUNTSMAN AND HOUNDS CROSSING A RIVER

Signed and dated 1909, Oil on canvas, 23 in by 28¼ in
Private collection

THE PATH TO THE ORCHARD

Signed and dated 1908, Oil on canvas, 29½ in by 42 in
Exhibited Royal Academy 1909
Collection: The Sir Alfred Munnings Art Museum

PONIES IN A SANDPIT

Signed. Painted 1911, Oil on canvas, 40 in by 50 in
Private collection

THE COMING STORM

Signed. Painted 1910, oil on canvas, 58⅜ in by 72 in
Exhibited Royal Academy 1925
Collection: New South Wales Art Gallery, Sydney, Australia

DONKEYS IN THE RINGLAND HILLS

Signed and dated 1911, Oil on canvas, 28 in by 37 in
Private collection

SHRIMP ON A WHITE WELSH PONY

Signed and dated 1911, Oil on canvas, 25 in by 30 in
Private collection

HUNTING MORNING

Signed and dated 1913, Oil on board, 20½ in by 26¼ in
Collection: The Sir Alfred Munnings Art Museum

GOING TO THE MEET

Signed. Painted 1913, Oil on canvas, 20 in by 24 in
Collection: Laing Municipal Art Gallery, Newcastle-upon-Tyne

THE DEPARTURE OF THE HOP-PICKERS

Signed. Painted 1913, Oil on canvas, 36 in by 40 in
Collection: National Gallery of Victoria, Melbourne, Australia

MAJOR-GENERAL THE RT. HON. J. E. B. SEELY

Signed. Painted 1918, Oil on canvas, 20 in by 24 in
Collection: Canadian War Museum, The National Museum of Man,
The National Museums of Canada, Ottawa

STRATHCONA'S HORSE ON THE MARCH

Signed. Painted 1918 Oil on canvas, 20 in by 24 in.
Collection: Canadian War Museum, The National Museum of Man,
The National Museums of Canada, Ottawa

FORT GARRY'S ON THE MARCH

Signed. Painted 1918, Oil on canvas, 20 in by 24 in
Collection: Canadian War Museum, The National Museum of Man,
The National Museums of Canada, Ottawa

MAJOR-GENERAL THE EARL OF ATHLONE

Signed. Painted 1919, Oil on canvas, 32 in by 28 in Exhibited Royal Academy 1920 Private collection

BELVOIR POINT-TO-POINT MEETING ON BARROWBY HILL

Signed. Painted 1920, Oil on canvas, 24½ in by 29½ in
Collection: Mr. and Mrs. Paul Mellon

Signed. Painted 1919, Oil on canvas, 34½ in by 50 in
Exhibited Royal Academy 1920
Collection: The Sir Alfred Munnings Art Museum

Signed. Painted 1920, Oil on canvas, 39½ in by 49½ in
Exhibited Royal Academy 1952
Collection: Aberdeen Art Gallery

EPSOM DOWNS. CITY AND SUBURBAN DAY

Signed. Painted 1919, Oil on canvas, 31¼ in by 50½ in
Exhibited Royal Academy 1920
Collection: The Tate Gallery, London

DRUM HORSE

Signed and dated 1922, Oil on canvas, 35 in by 36 in
Collection: The National Trust, Anglesey Abbey, Cambridgeshire

KILKENNY HORSE FAIR

Signed. Painted 1922, Oil on canvas, 24½ in by 29½ in
Exhibited Royal Academy 1923 and 1926 (Diploma Work, presented to the
Royal Academy on Munnings's election as an Academician in 1925)
Collection: The Royal Academy of Arts, London

THE GREY HORSE

Signed. 'Begun in 1913 and worked at again in 1923', Oil on canvas,
46 in by 56 in
Exhibited Royal Academy 1924
Collection: Mr. David Innes

FRANK FREEMAN ON 'PILOT'

Signed. Painted 1925, Oil on canvas, 39 in by 40 in
Exhibited Royal Academy 1929
Private collection

THE ASCOT PROCESSION CROSSING WINDSOR PARK

Signed. Painted 1925, Oil on canvas, 31 in by 42 in
Exhibited Royal Academy 1926
Reproduced by Gracious Permission of Her Majesty the Queen

ELEVEN O'CLOCK

Signed. Painted c.1932, Oil on canvas, 38 in by 42 in
Exhibited Royal Academy 1933
Collection: Mr. B. J. Eastwood

ON THE MOORS

Signed, Oil on canvas, 60 in by 48 in
Exhibited Royal Academy 1931
Collection: Mrs. Bing Crosby

Signed. Painted 1931, Oil on canvas, 22¾ in by 28¼ in
Exhibited Royal Academy 1932
Collection: Harris Museum and Art Gallery, Preston

MY WIFE, MY HORSE AND MYSELF

Signed. Painted 1932–3, Oil on canvas, 40 in by 50 in
Exhibited Royal Academy 1935
Collection: The Sir Alfred Munnings Art Museum

CHANGING HORSES

Signed. Painted 1920, Oil on canvas, 48 in by 72 in
Collection: Museum of Art, Carnegie Institute, Pittsburgh

Signed. Painted 1937, Oil on canvas, 20 in by 24 in
Exhibited Royal Academy 1938
Collection: The Earl of Derby

EARLY MORNING AT NEWMARKET
(THE HON. GEORGE LAMBTON AND HIS SON)

Signed. Oil on canvas, 37 in by 48 in
Exhibited Royal Academy 1929
Private collection

Signed and dated 1937, Oil on board, 13 in by 17 in
Private collection

IN THE UNSADDLING ENCLOSURE AT EPSOM

Painted c.1948, Oil on canvas, 26 in by 32⅞ in
Collection: The Sir Alfred Munnings Art Museum

STUDY OF A START AT NEWMARKET, 1951

Signed. Oil on panel, 18 in by 26 in
Collection: The Sir Alfred Munnings Art Museum

© 1986 The Castle House Trust

Published by Philip Wilson Publishers Limited
for Sotheby's Publications, 26 Litchfield Street,
London WC2H 9NJ

Available in the U.S.A. from Sotheby's Publications
Harper and Row, Publishers, Inc.,
10 East 53rd Street, New York NY 10022

ISBN 0 85667 347 1
LC 87-061924

Designed by Peter Ling
Filmset by Tradespools Limited, Frome, England
Printed by Graphicom, Vicenza, Italy

Erratum   Please note that illustration number 17,
Norwich Fair, should read as follows:

Susan at the Fair
Signed and dated 1908
Watercolour, heightened with bodycolour
12in by 15in
Collection: The Sir Alfred Munnings Art Museum